'JIM'
THE PAIN AND THE PASSION

The Story of

Watercolour Artist

James Merriott

Overcoming the pain and suffering

Of Rheumatoid Arthritis

by

Painting the Beauty of the World

DENT – YORKSHIRE DALES

Lord Ronald Rayner
Introduces
James Merriott

Very many people have within them a variety of artistic abilities. Unfortunately, for most of us, these abilities remain forever buried below the level of the conscious mind. For the lucky few however, these phenomenon well up in consciousness, driving men and women to produce the most powerful intuitively attractive representations of the beauty, the wonder and the awe of Planet Earth. Paintings, drawings and sketches that reveal something of the promise of even greater beauty that will be revealed in their works in Future Time. One of the lucky few is Artist James Merriott. His story reveals how his paintings were won from the efforts of mind, body, and spirit, working together as one.

Lord Ronald Rayner.

HUBBERHOLME – YORKSHIRE DALES

ST. MARY THE VIRGIN – BRENT PELHAM – HERTFORDSHIRE

YE OLD FIGHTING COCKS INN – HERTFORDSHIRE

THE BIRD IN HAND PUB – WESTMILL – HERTFORDSHIRE

LEMSFORD WATERMILL – HERTFORDSHIRE

THE WATERMILL

Listen to the watermill through the livelong
Day

How the clanking of its wheels wears the hours
Away

Languidly the autumn wind stirs the greenwood
Leaves

From the field the reapers sing, binding up their
Sheaves

And a proverb haunts my mind as a spell is
Cast

The mill cannot grind with water that is
Passed

Autumn wind revive no more, leaves that once are
Shed

And the sickle cannot reap, corn once
Gathered

Flow the ruffled streamlet on, tranquil, deep and
Still

Never gliding back again to the
Watermill

Truly speaks the proverb old, with a moaning
Vast

The mill cannot grind with water that is
Passed

Take the lesson to thy heart, through the loury
Heart

Golden youth is fleeing, summer hours
Depart

Learn to make the most of life, lose no happy
Day

Time will never bring thee back, chances swept
Away

Leave no tender word unsaid, love while love shall
Last

The mill cannot grind with water that is
Passed

Work while yet the daylight shines, man of
Strength and Will

Never does the streamlet glide, unless by the
Mill

Wait not till tomorrows, sun beams upon it's
Way

All that thou can'st call thine own, lies in thy
"Today"

Power and intellect and health, may not always
Last

The mill cannot grind with water that is
Passed

The wasted hours of life that have drifted
By

The good that might have been, lost without a
Sigh

Love that might have been once saved, by a single
Word

Thought conceived but never panned, perishing
Unheard

Take the proverb to thine heart, take and hold it
Fast

The mill cannot grind with water that is
Passed

John Valentine Alder

HOME PARK LOCK – KINGS LANGLEY – HERTFORDSHIRE

PERIGUEUX – DORDOGNE

BLACKTHORN PUBLISHING LTD.
UK & WORLDWIDE RETAIL DISTRIBUTORS & MANAGING AGENTS
EMAIL: lord.r.rayner@btinternet.com
TELEPHONE: (UK) 01621 743882

PUBLISHER
Blackthorn Publishing Ltd.,
Suite 404, Albany House,
324-326 Regent Street,
London, W1B 3HH,
United Kingdom.
EMAIL: lord.r.rayner@btinternet.com
TELEPHONE: (UK) 01621 743882

SPIRITUAL & METAPHYSICAL POETRY
THE BAND OF BROTHERS Chapter 6
By Sylvia Gladys Rayner
Lady of Annesley Grange, Notts

FOREWORD
Doctor Geoffrey Clarke M.A. MB B. CHIR. F.R.C.P.

EDITOR
Lord Ronald Rayner
Lord Carlton Lyndrick, Notts

GALLERY CONSULTANT
Darina Markovna Rayner

CREATIVE DESIGN
Craig Allen Rayner
Lord Kilvington, Notts
ISBN: 9780 9557 90676

PRINTERS
Colt Press Ltd., Unit 7C Perry Road, Witham, Essex, CM3 3UD, United Kingdom.

DEDICATION

Dedicated to my wife Joan and children Julie and Richard. Their love, care and encouragement has sustained my Spirit.

ACKNOWLEDGEMENTS

Words all but fail me to acknowledge my gratitude to Lord Ronald Rayner, Sylvia Gladys Rayner and their son Craig Allen Rayner, for without them this book would not have been possible. Their belief has encouraged me enormously and their commitment has been exceptional.

My very special thanks to Craig, who spent endless hours designing my 'mish mash' of words and watercolours into something beautiful.

To record also my gratitude to so many other people who have encouraged me is perhaps the hardest task of all. I can therefore only try and apologise to so many friends that I am unable to mention.

To Colin Ayers who's companionship is very special. Richard and Lorraine who I have been able to rely upon more than anybody else to visit my exhibitions all the way from Cambridgeshire. They must now have more watercolours than wall space.

To all my painting partners who come to my home and teach me more about painting than I teach them.

To Dr. Geoffrey Clarke and George Taylor for their kind comments and invaluable contributions. To Bill Newman for his masterpiece of me motorcycle racing at Brands Hatch in 1965, who with Sylvia's beautiful words 'Band of Brothers' produced such a remarkable and moving contribution of poetry and painting.

The brilliant Ian Brown for his super caricature, in which he made me look far more handsome than I really am.

My thanks also to Author Sylvia Kent who has been greatly encouraging.

Last but not least my wife Joan and family for their understanding and who between them keep me going in something like the right direction.

FOOTNOTE

The text in this book has been compiled from a lifetime of memories, and although the facts and sequence of events are true as I remember them, it is inevitable that some inaccuracies may have occurred.

CHAPTER INDEX

INGATESTONE HALL – ESSEX

THE HOME OF LORD PETRE – LORD LIEUTENANT OF ESSEX – LAUNCHED THIS BOOK ON 22 JULY 2011

'JIM'
By
George

LIVING THIS LIFE IS LIVING A DREAM, THIS IS SIMPLY THE
BEST IT COULD HAVE BEEN

IT IS SOMETHING HE WOULD NOT HAVE MISSED, BEING A
WATER COLOURIST

SPENDING HIS TIME IN DIFFERENT PLACES, VILLAGE
STREETS OPEN SPACES

A PICTURE FINISHED THEN IT'S SIGNED, A LITTLE PIECE OF
HIM LEFT BEHIND

WHILE STRUGGLING WITH ARTHRITIC HANDS, AND ALL THE
PROBLEMS THIS LIFE DEMANDS

YET ALWAYS OPEN, ALWAYS SHARING, DESPITE THE PAIN
HE IS BEARING

BUT HE COULDN'T MANAGE THIS ON HIS OWN, THERE
WOULDN'T BE JIM IF IT WASN'T FOR JOAN

HELPING HIM BUILD HIS LEGACY, TO LEAVE BEHIND FOR THE
WORLD TO SEE

A MAN CONTENTED WITH HIS LOT, MY ARTIST FRIEND
JAMES MERRIOTT

G.S.TAYLOR

JIM'S CARICATURE
by
IAN BROWN

INTRODUCTION

The poem 'JIM' was presented to me in 2008 by a new found friend 'George'. At the time George had suffered the loss of his wife Lorraine, who died of cancer aged 59. He sought some heart ease by writing his beautiful poetry. 'JIM' was one of many and remains a much cherished part of my life.

In 1971 I was diagnosed with chronic Rheumatoid Arthritis and for the next 40 years have been battered with cruel pain and aggressive deformity of both hands.

The good news was that the disease was not terminal and was to direct me into a life of love and beauty. Even better news was that I was to be cared for over many years by Dr. Clarke.

I first returned to painting in 1973 while serving as a professional fire-fighter in the London Fire Brigade. I was inspired by the work of the late Gordon Benningfield (1936-1998), and completed a watercolour of a Blue Tit, the first I had done since my 'O' level work in 1957 and the first of many thousands that were to follow.

From those early paintings I learned that the tasks would not be easy, but each time I experienced severe pain, I hit back first with one watercolour and then another and so found myself at the beginning of my 'journey' recording beauty from all over Europe. A journey of learning, progress and improvement, and best of all a journey through life without any need to reach targets.

Painting has brought me into contact with many wonderful friends, and without doubt it is those friends that I am most indebted. It is for them that I complete this book.

This then, in that over written introduction to many books is 'My Story'. One that in spite of that diagnosis in 1971, has been filled to the brim with so many wonderful times and good fortune. A lifetime that has been a continuous flow of lucky breaks.

James Merriott

CHATEAU LACYPIERRE – ST. CREPIN – DORDOGNE

CHAPTER 1

MY HOME PATCH

I have always considered myself to be a countryman, albeit I was born in the East End of London. My birthplace, Clapton E8, was more country than city, being only yards from the River Lea and Lea Marshes.

As a small boy I marvelled at the sight of Sticklebacks and Newts, which, with my young brother Steve, we caught in a drag net from local ponds and canals. Victoria (Vicky) Park, Wanstead Park and the canal at Gunmakers lane, Bow, gave us everything we ever needed, discovering the natural world at a time long before the days of hysteria television and noisy computer games.

I remain eternally grateful to Steve (15-02-1943 to 12-09-09) who was a far better brother to me than I ever was to him. Steve was a beautiful human being and a brilliant engineer. A superb artist in his own right, who could cut through stone with hammer and bolster with the skill of a master mason. Every single person, I believe, leaves a legacy.

My early infant years were spent living in a wonderful old cottage as an evacuee at Brent Eleigh in Suffolk. After the war my countryman claims took a severe nosedive when we moved to Poplar near the Gas Works at Stink House Bridge, and then to Bow opposite the asbestos factory.

I was however, always able to venture out into 'my' countryside on my sisters 'hand me down' bike. I remember that I had to stand as I peddled as I was too small to reach the seat. On this 'just about manageable form of transport' I discovered Wanstead Flats and Whipps Cross.

My father once asked me "Jimmy, where have you been all day?" I replied with a sense of great achievement, "To the countryside dad". Putting it mildly, I received a severe telling off.

At the age of eleven I became a paper boy delivering newspapers, and was able to save enough money to buy a real bicycle with dropped handlebars and a container with a straw which meant you could sip as you cycled!! Best of all I fitted a gadget to the front wheel that clocked up the miles I did.

Now I was really mobile and discovered Epping Forest and treasures further afield; the villages of Chigwell and Abridge, in a landscape I regard as my area of outstanding natural beauty.

Just upstream from Abridge on the River Roding lies the weather boarded Passingford Bridge Watermill, and my love of both the mill and river remains to this day. The last miller at Passingford was Bill Twynham. Sad to say that since Bill passed away some years back, the mill has declined into a state of disrepair. Perhaps even at this eleventh hour somebody will resurrect it into the building that it once was.

PASSINGFORD BRIDGE WATERMILL – RIVER RODING – ESSEX

Married to Joan in 1967 we settled in Brentwood where we have remained to this day. We often drive past the mill and Joan has come to love it as much as me.

CURTIS MILL GREEN

Only a matter of yards from Passingford Mill, Curtis Mill Green, leads to a remnant of Waltham Forest that takes the traveller back in time.

Among the many ancient cottages here is 'Willow Cottage' perhaps the best kept secret in Essex. Mr Williams and his wife purchased the 17th century cottage in 1953, when it had for centuries remained exactly as it did when built. The new owners safeguarded its history and maintained it in its original condition into the 21st century.

Adjoining the cottage, a natural amphitheatre was discovered in 1962. To this day plays and concerts are held throughout the summer months in what must be the prettiest settings of any theatre in England.

Willow Cottage is featured in the DVD 'My Way with Watercolour'.

WILLOW COTTAGE – ESSEX

HADLEIGH CASTLE – ESSEX

4

BRIDGE COTTAGE – VALE OF DEDHAM – CONSTABLE COUNTRY

DEDHAM – ESSEX

FLATFORD WATER MILL

WILLY LOTTS COTTAGE – FLATFORD

MOUNTNESSING POST WINDMILL – ESSEX

THE TIDE MILL – WOODBRIDGE – SUFFOLK

BARGES ON THE RIVER ORWELL – SUFFOLK

TOWER BRIDGE – RIVER THAMES

CHAPTER 2

I HAVE REASON TO BELIEVE IN MIRACLES

There is one moment in my life that stands out as more important than any other. It was 1976 when I attended my first Rheumatology clinic under our National Health Service.

I waited to be called into the consultancy room, desperate for help, because over the five years or so since being diagnosed, I had become weak and crippled; at times with excruciating pain.

"Good grief man, how long have you been like that?" Dr. Geoffrey Clark commented as I entered the room. He then promised me two things by saying, "You'll not now suffer as much as you have in the past, and that I can do so much to help your mobility".

Throughout the many years that followed my first meeting with this really great man, I was to be treated by him countless times.

I could write this whole book on the incredible results I received from his skills, especially treating all my joints with cortisone injections, but suffice to say the very next day following that first treatment I was able to walk without pain.

At 70 years of age, I can best sum up the reality of what happened to me with a line from a Bob Dylan song, 'My Back Pages',

"I was so much older then, I'm younger than that now"

ST. PETERS CHURCH – COLCHESTER – ESSEX

DR. G. R. CLARKE

M.A. MB B. CHIR. F.R.C.P.

It is a great privilege to be invited to write a foreword for James Merriott. In rising to the challenge to write his book, Jim is doing a service to all the many people who suffer from (broadly speaking) musculoskeletal disorders amongst which arthritis, often generalised, is prominent.

Most medical conditions have a tendency to isolate or alienate people from the things they hold dear. Widespread arthritis, such as we may see in rheumatoid arthritis is very liable to do this. 'No man is an island' wrote John Donne, but a person with arthritis may feel increasingly that one is just that, an island, cut off from the normal supplies of life. To depart from the island and back to mainland living is essentially a team process. Each person, in varying degrees, can be enabled to make a creative response to what is usually a painful intrusion into their lives. This response depends on a variety of factors. For example, how well they are able to relate to family and medical team, and vice versa, and the extent to which this interaction can help them to achieve their life hopes and aspirations.

TEWIN CHURCH – HERTFORDSHIRE

WRITTLE – ESSEX

I first met Jim some 35 years ago. I had just started as consultant in Rheumatology to the Havering District. This speciality of medicine was emerging as an increasingly scientific discipline from more primitive origins. As such, there was a lot of work to be done to help patients who had not seen a Rheumatologist, and to ensure that there were adequate resources to deal with the size of the problem. In both these Jim figured prominently. He had already endured arthritis for 7 years. Nowadays, to give an idea of how far we have come both in the sense of urgency needed to properly manage arthritis, and to ensure early diagnosis and treatment, we consider three months from the start of symptoms to be erring on the late side.

In some people there is a more gradual development, so that some joints come on later. In Jim's case the hands and feet had already become adversely affected with elements of permanent loss of function. These peripheral joints remain a challenge. Even so, Jim has adapted his style of painting to the obstinacy of the stiff and angulated hand joints. But his knees were more recent and these responded very well to treatment back in 1976, so that, by and large, he has maintained his lower limb function. Very important when one considers the joy Jim gets from painting in the open, and discovering the detail of his subjects. So the lesson is, there is always something we can do for all, whatever the stage of their first visit. It is always going to be useful to the individual concerned.

16

Jim's story illustrates another important aspect of the arthritis journey, namely that one has to be always on the look-out for accompanying conditions that may affect mobility or general health. For example, it is not generally known that certain types of arthritis can cause anaemia. However, approximately two out of three people have an additional cause for the condition. Other experts to whom I referred him did not seem to think he had a problem at first, but we persevered with this symptom in Jim's case and were finally rewarded by diagnosing his gluten allergy. Directly this was treated, his anaemia disappeared and Jim's general health, especially energy, improved. That energy has been a very important part of his ability to pour out his paintings.

WALKERN WATER MILL – HERTFORDSHIRE

17

SIBLE HEDINGHAM WATERMILL – ESSEX

Jim is undoubtedly an enthusiast in painting in watercolour, and he and some wonderful friends brought this to bear on the other side of the equation, namely to provide resources which, clearly, the NHS could not. Soon a committee comprising friends and patients, all truly committed, were meeting regularly, and arranging numerous fund raising events, large and small, plus starting a registered charity called 'Forth'.

Year after year, for several years, Jim painted a local scene for exclusive Christmas Cards that sold and sold (10,000 in 1988). At this rate it was not long before we had sufficient funds to appoint salaried staff, a specialist nurse in rheumatology (the first in Essex), a Senior House Officer, and part-time staff including a physiotherapist and clerical assistant. Imagine what a difference all this made. After 3 years the NHS saw the importance and put them on the payroll, paving the foundations for better care.

New treatments have been introduced, and care standards have been sharpened over the years, but the fight continues to ensure delivery of resources that are possible, in a timely way. Given early referral, there is every chance now to achieve lasting remission, which, though usually undergirded by regular medication, and careful follow-up, in many cases, amounts to a cure. Others gain at least a stable situation, enabling a better framework to live more confident and creative lives. It is no wonder that rheumatologists across the UK have, over the past three decades at least, been determined to provide a world class service for their patients. Currently, this involves dialogue and presentations to those involved with the present NHS reorganisation, in order to ensure the needs of this large group of people is not marginalised.

ST. MARYS CHURCH – WENDENS AMBO – ESSEX

HEDINGHAM CASTLE – ESSEX

During his life Jim's career changed course a number of times, but there was always a logical pattern; a creative response to the level of mobility he could achieve. Painting, especially from the 1980's, was always simmering away until rather like a butterfly emerging from its chrysalis, the true raison d'être for his presence here on Earth came out with an increasing flow of pictures to please us all. He himself remains spurred on by that inner urge to experiment, giving vent to that essentially spiritual force within that has delighted us even more.

The possibility of loss of function is always a threat with arthritis, especially if it is not treated quickly enough, which may in some ways acts to give a sense of urgency. This leads an individual to think and explore themselves more deeply to find what lies within, and bring it out. Recently, a patient about to have a potentially painful procedure, became calm, telling me she was saying over in her mind the serenity prayer, "Oh God, grant me the serenity to accept the things I cannot change, the courage to change the things I can, and the wisdom to know the difference". I thanked her for reminding me of the prayer, and we thank Jim and Joan who became as far as is humanly possible the living embodiment of that prayer.

CHAPTER 3

BEAUTIFUL BRITAIN

Until 1985 I had no desire to ever leave these islands, and to the annoyance of my family I never did, except at Easter 1960 when I went with my amateur football team to play in Belgium. We played one game and were thrashed 6-2, but then you can't be good at everything.

My needs, I believe, were very simple, the need to hear the song of a Blackbird or Thrush outside my window before I left for work each morning (my first profession was that of a Cabinet Maker, happily making handmade furniture).

Like millions of others I have benefited from modern life, which has enabled me to travel not only in Britain but in the latter years to Europe.

The beauty and diversity of these islands is quite unparalleled, and I do at times wonder if I have been dreaming.

The rugged coves of Cornwall, the vast skies of East Anglia, the magnificence of mountain views of Scotland, Wales, Ireland, and those I love most, the English Lake District.

Add to these the Dales of Yorkshire and Derbyshire, the Cotswolds and the Chilterns etc. Do I need to say more.

I do then have much to be enthralled by, to love and appreciate, the landscapes of Britain, landscapes I was born to.

MORSTON QUAY - NORFOLK

KINGFISHER

THE ROUND HOUSE – SENNEN COVE – CORNWALL

RIVER LEA AT WARE – HERTFORDSHIRE

WOODBRIDGE TIDE MILL – SUFFOLK

'THE VIPER INN' FRYERNING – ESSEX

BRIDGE OF SIGHS – CAMBRIDGESHIRE

ANCIENT PORT OF MALDON – ESSEX

ELVET BRIDGE – DURHAM

NATURAL COLLECTION OF HANDMADE PAPERS FROM MOULIN DE LARROQUE, FRANCE

ST. ANDREWS CHURCH – GREENSTED – ONGAR – ESSEX

ASHNESS BRIDGE – LAKE DISTRICT

WAST WATER – LAKE DISTRICT

WATENDLATH – LAKE DISTRICT

ST. JOHNS VALE – LAKE DISTRICT

Prests Mill
ColdBeck
1 8 - 03 - 10

PRIESTS MILL CALDBECK – LAKE DISTRICT

HUBBERHOLME – YORKSHIRE

HANDMADE DRAWING PAPER FROM THE MOULIN DE LARROQUE, COUZE ST. FRONT, DORDOGNE

MALHAM POST OFFICE – YORKSHIRE DALES

LOWER SLAUGHTER – COTSWOLDS

CHAPTER 4

ESSEX AND HERTFORDSHIRE
LIFE MAGAZINES

We have a dear friend who visits us frequently. He telephones first with always the same introduction "Hello Jim and Joan, this is Dennis here from West Horndon", we find this delightful and a little amusing.

He visited on one occasion during the autumn of 2004 and gave us 5 volumes of the Essex Countryside magazines, dating back to the late 1960's to early 1970's. These Dennis said, you can keep on permanent loan and this I accepted with pleasure and have kept them ever since.

The magazine originated in 1952 at the same time that I was discovering the countryside. I can remember seeing these beautiful locations depicted in colour on front covers of these magazines displayed in newsagents shops. I was greatly inspired to visit these places myself.

I have spent many hours relishing the contents of those loaned to me by Dennis.

FOOTPATH STEPS – ALBURY – HERTFORDSHIRE

WALNUT TREE FARMHOUSE – PIRTON – HERTFORDSHIRE

Of those many features published almost 50 years ago, one series delighted me more than most. This was a country walk in the county, but more importantly it was illustrated with the paintings of Leonard Wyatt. How I loved, even drooled over these paintings. Wonderful places that I had come to know so well and loved so much.

It is absolutely unrelated and quite an amazing coincidence that early in 2005 I received an invitation from the Essex Life magazine (as it is now called) to become resident featured artist.

I was both astonished and incredibly excited, and it took a little time for it to dawn on me that I had received an invitation that quite simply was the biggest thing in my life as an artist. Shortly after I was invited to illustrate in the Hertfordshire Life magazine, and have continued to this present time.

I have always visited lovely places for the thrill of seeing the beauty and to draw and paint. Since my first issue in April 2005, the objective has had more purpose. Not only do I continue to visit and portray the villages of Essex and Hertfordshire, and share them with the readers, but also bring pleasure in the same way Leonard Wyatt had brought to me.

THE WOODEN DOOR – EARLS COLNE – ESSEX
PAINTED ON A VERY ROUGH PAPER

41

BRIDGE END – NEWPORT – ESSEX

BURY CHASE COTTAGE – FELSTED – ESSEX

HIGH STREET SHOPS – WELWYN – HERTFORDSHIRE

HIGH STREET – WALTON ON THE NAZE – ESSEX

FOLLY COTTAGE – ALDBURY – HERTFORDSHIRE

COTTAGES ON THE QUAY – WIVENHOE – ESSEX

COCKLE SHEDS – LEIGH ON SEA – ESSEX

THE JOLLY SWAGMAN NARROWBOAT – GRAND UNION CANAL – BERKHAMSTED – HERTFORDSHIRE

BROCKET PARK – LEMSFORD – HERTFORDSHIRE

COTTAGE BY THE GREEN – KIMPTON – HERTFORDSHIRE

THE GREAT GATEWAY OF THE MONASTERY – ST. ALBANS – HERTFORDSHIRE

CHAPTER 5

SCOTLAND, IRELAND AND JACK MERRIOTT

Joan and I are privileged to visit many art clubs and groups throughout the county, and beyond, to complete watercolour demonstrations and 'Paint along with' workshops.

One question comes up time and time again, 'Are you related to the famous Jack Merriott?' I am immensely proud to respond, 'Indeed I am'.

Jack Merriott was a very great artist. The commissioned work he undertook was of the highest order. He was present in Westminster Abbey to record, as it happened, in pencil and then paint the Coronation of Queen Elizabeth II. He completed many paintings for the (National) General Post Office, depicting Post Offices throughout Britain, but perhaps his greatest triumph was to become the most celebrated artist to complete poster and carriage panels for the various Railway Companies.

Authentic panels and prints are now collector's items, and I am fortunate to have inherited a limited number of panels through my family.

Among the 10 given to me by Mrs Hilda Merriott, were 5 portraying the Highlands of Scotland. These awesome views portrayed so magnificently were inspiration to see the same locations myself. On my first visit I immediately realised that painting such vast vistas of beauty proved the hardest subjects I have ever tackled. The big problem being the continuing changing light, something Jack had handled with seemingly ultimate ease.

PACK HORSE BRIDGE – SCOTTISH HIGHLANDS

I have only been to Ireland once, but realised a lifetime dream, visiting the Ring of Kerry, and Beara in the South West. I instantly became totally captivated by these magnificent landscapes that remain completely unaffected by time.

After painting many watercolours of Scotland and Ireland I continue to return to those by Jack, and remain enchanted by the magnitude of his work, and my feet are kept firmly on the ground.

Jack Merriott 1901 – 1968, was Vice President of the Royal Institute of Painters in Watercolour, member of the Royal Institute of Painters in Oil, member of the Royal Society of Marine Artists and a member of The Pastel Society. Jack was also a founder member of The Wapping Group of Artists, and a member of the prestigious Langham Group. He was paramount in a group of exceptionally talented water colourists who lived and worked during the middle of the last century.

Water colour is a very English medium, and the brilliance of the work these men produced is not likely to ever be repeated.

OLD CROFT BY THE ROAD – RING OF KERRY – SOUTHERN IRELAND

'THE COBBLER' AND LOCH LONG – SCOTLAND

BRIDGE OF BALGIE – GLEN LYON – SCOTLAND

BALLYCARBERY CASTLE – RING OF KERRY – SOUTHERN IRELAND

BALLYCROVANE HARBOUR – RING OF BEARA – SOUTHERN IRELAND

LOCH ARKLET – SCOTTISH HIGHLANDS

AN OLD CROFT – RING OF BEARA – SOUTHERN IRELAND

CHAPTER 6

TRIUMPH AND TRAGEDY

Since my age of reasoning there has not been a single day in my life when the love of art has not been with me.

Life however does at times take other avenues with tragic circumstances. The loss of loved ones is always so hard to bear and never is the loss so tragic than when a loved one dies very young.

The paintings left to the world by both Vincent Van Gogh 1853 – 1890 and Henri Toulouse Lautrec 1864 – 1901 have become the most loved of all.

Both men alas lived unhappy lives and died in their thirties. Their triumph however lives on forever.

Both Richard Parkes Bonnington 1802 – 1828 and Thomas Girtin 1775 – 1802 at first found triumph in that they produced so many watercolour masterpieces, but tragedy in that they died when only 26 and 27.

It is, I believe, the human spirit that causes man to pitch himself against the limits of endurance and to take risks. Through the media I have witnessed the flights to the Moon, the climbing of Mount Everest and yachts being sailed single handed around the World.

In 1964 I borrowed £250.00 from my father, negotiated buying a Manx Norton Road Racing Motorcycle, and a clapped out banger van to transport it. I went off to Brands Hatch and did a few laps and said to myself, "Yes! I'm a Road Racer". Although I spent the summer of 1965 racing at many circuits, nothing has remained of my racing memorabilia, except for a few action photographs. Nothing, that is, but memories.

During July that year I entered the "Stars of Tomorrow" Road Race meeting at Brands Hatch. The 350cc event was a terrific race, won brilliantly by Rod Lee only yards ahead of 5 or 6 of us fellow competitors who followed him over the line.

On August Bank Holiday Monday I was back at Brands, but it was different, very different. I found myself on the 3rd row of the grid amid some of the Greatest Road Racers in the World.

In the silence before the start, Murray Walker became very excited, as he always did, reading out the names of the top stars on the front row and relishing the prospect of a magnificent race. I had a great start and managed to hang on in there 'holding my own with the pack' and although I don't think I did anything wrong, halfway through the race I lost it, and was dumped unceremoniously onto the tarmac at 'Clearways'. I was bitterly disappointed, but very lucky to be OK, so picked myself up to fight another day.

Another day came at Snetterton some weeks later. Everyone was there again including myself and Rod Lee. The 350cc junior event, as it was called, was divided into heats with competition to qualify for the Final. My heat finished, I went to watch the 2nd from the pits where the terrible news came through of a very bad fall. Like I had done at Brands, Rod had fallen while racing on the limit. His injuries were severe and he died in hospital a few days after the crash. Just one of us young men in our prime doing what we loved doing, taking part in the wonderful sport of Motor Cycle Road Racing.

On the morning of the 28th February 1975, the 08:37 tube train from Drayton Park packed with commuters rammed into a dead end at the end of the platform at Moorgate underground station. The carnage was catastrophic and fire crews from throughout London, together with police, paramedics, doctors, nurses and blood transfusion teams fought day long to free from the wreckage, those that could be saved.

At 18:00 hours I reported for Duty at Shoreditch Fire Station, and was one of many ordered on to relieve exhausted crews at the scene. There was no hesitation, indeed crews competed with one another for positive positions from where they could help. I relieved my old mate Richard 'Twizzle' Furlong in a part of the wreckage with two people still trapped. They proved to be the last persons to be rescued alive.

The following few hours were the most dramatic and moving moments of my life. Above all I witnessed enormous courage, not by rescuers, but by those trapped. Those two people, side by side in the wreckage, were a young woman Police Officer and a young man. It was a massive struggle to free them. As we worked, we talked a lot to each other about life, we also talked to fellow rescuers in different positions below but obscured from our view by wreckage.

Eventually the moment of elation came, due mainly to the skill of a surgeon. The moment of triumph was dampened that the young lady had lost part of her leg. The release of the young man followed shortly after, he was apparently completely unharmed. We fire crews and medical staff spontaneously broke into rapturous applause and cheering as he was manoeuvred to freedom. He shook hands with all of us as we continued to cheer his departure.

The young police woman made a good recovery and I believe continued her work at administrative duties in the police force.

Forty one people had died that day, but fate had not yet finished. The young man, we learned from reports had died in hospital a few weeks after that fateful day, the 42nd victim of the Moorgate Tube Train Disaster. The report ended that he died after putting up a magnificent fight for life. He was 26 years old. We who had taken part in his rescue were devastated, and could only ask ourselves one thing, 'why? Why, indeed!

THE BAND OF BROTHERS

Yes my friend.
We left the world behind.
Never to return.

Time stood still and Jupiter in her
Positive way took on our challenge.
Saturn took us by the hand.
The Band of Brothers.

Our dreams fulfilled as we
Entered Time and Space.
On and on journeying as one
Our New World.
Our New Beginning.

Sylvia Gladys Rayner

The beauty, commitment and comradeship is epitomised in this magnificent pastel painting from my great friend and fellow artist Bill Newman.

It commemorates a memorable part of my life. (My Racing Number that day was No.6). The Painting depicts Druids Hill at Brands Hatch, on a July day in 1965.

The Race was won by No.22 Rod Lee, who sadly lost his life at a meeting shortly afterwards.

COMMISSIONED PASTEL PAINTING BY BILL NEWMAN

64

As I Said at the Beginning
My Life is Full
of
Lucky Breaks

The older I become the more I remember these two men that died so young, Rod Lee and Jeff. Although we met only briefly, how fortunate I was to have known them both.

'Twizzle' was awarded the British Empire Medal for services at Moorgate. It was a recognition of everyone who took part in the rescue operation including the staff at Brigade Control and all those crews on standby.

This was a very proud time in the history of the London Fire Brigade which functions as a team. I retired from service in March 1978 and remain privileged to have served with such wonderful colleagues and to have been part of that team.

As for the road racing, following Rod's tragic death, I finished my remaining races during that year and gave up the sport. However road racing in the 1960's was racing in the Golden Years and, again I am privileged to have taken part.

I have no regrets, and remain mindful that a well turned out Road Racing Motorcycle in the hands of an expert is beauty in motion. An art form demanding touch, timing and courage, in rather the same way as does a good watercolour. Get it wrong and there's no second chance.

Following retirement from the London Fire Brigade, an amazing turn of fortune followed. I was knocked off my bicycle by a car on a dark wet night, which led to the driver putting me in touch with the Plant Protection manager who employed me as an in house fireman with the Ford Motor Company at a new office building in Brentwood. I retired on the 31st December 1992 after 13 very happy years with Ford.

During this time I began to make progress with my painting and drawing and from then on I was to dedicate the remainder of my life to the pleasures of art.

ARDLEIGH – ESSEX

66

BONNYMEAD COTTAGE - BRENT PELHAM - HERTFORDSHIRE

ST. MARTINS CHURCH – LITTLE WALTHAM – ESSEX

SOUTH HANNINGFIELD CHURCH – ESSEX

ST. ANDREW AND ST. MARY
WATTON AT STONE – HERTFORDSHIRE

CHAPTER 7

FRANCE, ITALY
AND
JOHN CONSTABLE

These landscapes made me a painter so said John Constable 1776 – 1837, speaking of his native Vale of Dedham. It is easy to see why he said it, for these breathtaking views are quite simply the finest painting subjects on Earth. I myself, never tire of this timeless countryside and live near enough to be able to call it my local painting area.

As well as his oils, Constable was a watercolour genius and like many others, I have been greatly influenced by him. So, what was it that made me paint the way I do? In a word – France! Or to be more precise that part of France I know as 'le Perigord' or the Dordogne.

From mighty Chateaux to tiny pigeonnier, I adore the golden sandstone used to build these amazing structures, the material is as golden as a wedding ring placed on the finger of a bride, and over the years I taught myself a way of portraying it.

PIGEONNIER JAVERLHAC – DORDOGNE

CHATEAU MARTHONIE – ST. JEAN DE COLE

72

PIGEONNIER – DORDOGNE

I used lots of water and added yellow ochre, light red and cobalt blue to establish the colour of the golden stone, and more often than not just waited for the magic to happen. My style was born!!

Of course it wasn't just the style in France, I found so much more. The fields of sunflowers, the wild flower meadows with their cascades of poppies, the hospitality of the people, the sun, the sheer tranquillity, the language and of course the endless fields of vineyards, producing perhaps the very best of what is France – the wines. France not only made me a water colourist, but also appreciative of fine wines.

We return year after year to the same area. Always, there are new discoveries and a sense of belonging within this most majestic of landscapes. It has captivated me, I dream it.

Any country that has cities the like of Rome, Venice and Florence, how does the modern painter cope, especially when he has been preceded by the greatest of the greats, Michael Angelo, Leonardo de Vinci, Canaletto and Raphael to name only a few.

The secret is to cherish each moment, feel privileged to follow in the footsteps of such great masters, whether it be Canaletto in Venice or Constable in the Vale of Dedham. These monumental places are more than just a beauty, they are the very spirits of the great artist that immortalised them. Their presence will remain as long as such places exist.

73

BUSSIERE BADIL – DORDOGNE

LE MOULIN SOUS LE ROC – COUZE ET SAINT FRONT – VILLAGE PAPIER – DORDOGNE

CHATEAU DE ROCHEBRUNE – POITOU CHARENTES

PONT MEDIEVAL – LE CHALARD – DORDOGNE

HOTEL CHASSAING – SARLAT – DORDOGNE

RESTAURANT IN SARLAT – DORDOGNE

PEN DRAWING OF CHAPDEUIL – DORDOGNE
HANDMADE PAPER SPECKLED WITH FLOWER PETALS

SAINT EMILION

Sketched in 1989 – Painted in 2009

MONPAZIER

Sketched in 1989 – Painted in 2009

ST. JEAN DE COLE – DORDOGNE

CHATEAU DE PANISSEAU

COLLE – VAL D'ELSA – TUSCANY – ITALY

GONDALAS AND THE ISLAND OF GIUDECCA – VENICE – ITALY

CHAPTER 8

THE OTHER SIDE OF THE STILE
SOME EARLY WORKS

I t's often said to me by my fellow painting companions, "I'd love to paint as loose as you". My style is positively loose, or to put it another way, a direct statement with paint without fussy detail. Loose! I am now, but it wasn't always like that and it has taken many years of practise and perseverance.

I struggled so much to achieve atmospheric landscapes, I first concentrated on wildlife art. My efforts to improve included producing a wildlife diary in 1985. The complete works I have retained in its entirety, and some of the paintings and drawings from that volume are reproduced here.

Stile under Yew
Hutton Village

J. Merriott 14·12·85

I had intended to start my entries in this book at the beginning of 1986, but a visit to the R.S.P.B. reserve at Minsmere on the last day of November 1985 caused me to become impatient to start. So my book begins :-

Minsmere - 30th November 1985

My companions on this, my first visit to Minsmere, were my nephew - Mike, whos knowledge of birds surpasses mine, and my son - Richard, aged 8, whos energy surpasses everyones. It was an overcast day but mild and it kept dry throughout.

My first impression of the reserve was what an out standing variation of habitat it contained. The waterways on the outskirts of the reserve brought anticipation of what would follow. There was however a setback, we found the reserve closed.

It made little difference as we watched the birds from the National Trust hide on the opposite side. From here we watched Waders, Gulls and Ducks, saw a Kingfisher flash past on 3 or 4 occasions, had just a glimpse of a Heron as it landed behind shrub and heard but could not see a stonechat. No Harriers were seen, but a Kestrel hovering over different areas of the reserve for much of the time was seen to dive on one occasion. Later a walk along a riverbank was highlighted by flocks of Redpoles and Goldfinches seen feeding from Alder trees.

Black-headed
Gull.

Wigeon

Great
black-backed
gull.

Shoveler

Wigeon

Drawn from sketches completed
in the public hide at Minsmere
on 30th November 1985

J. Merriott
7-12-85

JM 13·12·85

9th December 1985

Because it can be seen every day of the year in my garden and with it featuring on so many christmas cards at this time, should surely have been reason enough to want to paint a Robin. I did in fact have another reason, when I went out to Hutton Village to find and sketch a stile for the title page of my book, the local 'churchyard' Robin became my companion for the hour. As I sketched I pondered a 'Redbreast thought' or two. "No other occupant from our countryside can be more well known or better loved. At all times and in all places it presents itself as a wonderful example of the joy to be found in the creatures with whom we share this land."

The Robin and the sketch were not the only pleasant moments of the afternoon. I watched lapwings fly in onto farmland where they shared the fields with gulls and on my walk home I saw my first fieldfare of the winter as it flew across Hutton Warren. The Warren is a lovely tree surrounded meadow, seemingly put to no use by its owner but much appreciated by local residents and wildlife inhabitants alike.

J Merriott
20·12·85

19th December 1985

A visit to the Warren excelled in that 27 species of birds were seen. Redwing and Fieldfare, Magpie and Jay, Yellowhammer and Reed bunting in the Warren with many Wrens, more seen than ever before. A hundred or more Lapwings were on the adjoining farmland and a Kestrel flew from the trees in the churchyard. It was however not the birds that gave me my most captivating moments—It was the sky. It was one of those days of winter purity. A dazzling bright sky set the pasture where the horses were grazing aglow with winter colour. I sat on a fallen oak and as I sketched the horses I watched the sky cascade into colour as the afternoon drew to a close. Such splendid tranquillity was reflected in the engaging movements of the animals.

Magpie

Wren

Reed Bunting

Fieldfare

J Merriott
26-12-85

Birds in the Warren
19th December 1985

Yellowhammer

Jay

Bullfinch

Redwing

J Merriott
23·12·85

Thorndon Park - 27th December 1985

J Merriott
30·12·8

The Red Fox

27th December 1985

The first day of this christmas holiday season that was available to me was a lovely clear bright day and encouraged by my daughter Julie, who was keen to use her new camera, I decided to go to my local Thorndon Park. To complete the family outing my wife Joan and Richard also came.

Everybody complained of cold feet but our reward for braving the bite of a crisp north wind was to see a Red Fox, first time I'd seen a fox at Thorndon Park. His golden winter coat was immaculate, glowing under the bright winter sun. At the same time that we saw him, he also saw us and he at once lifted himself off the footpath with the ease of water running from a tap. The snow white tip of his tail was the last we saw as he disappeared into the vegitation.

Later, on the approach to Childerditch Common in the car, we were met by another surprise. A large male Pheasant insisted that I slow down to allow him to cross the road and as if by gratitude he stayed by the roadside just long enough to be admired by all, then he, like the fox earlier, was gone into the undergrowth

Pheasant   JM 31·12·85

95

Great Tit.

Blue Tit.

J Merriott 4·1·86

29th December 1985

Because of the bitterly cold weather it was very necessary to put out food for the wild birds. I filled 4 containers with peanuts, 2 mesh a stocking and a spindle, and hung them in the garden. Blue Tits are always present on the nuts but the Great Tits are seen less often. Great Tits however as well as the Blue Tits were seen feeding on the spindle of peanuts today.

Greenfinch

Greenfinches are other
birds that can be seen
every day feeding on the peanuts.

A rarer garden visitor, the
Pied wagtail fed among
scraps put out on the
garage roof next
door, on the first
day of 1986

Pied
Wagtail

J. Merriott
5.1.86

Birds in the
Garden
29.12.85 to 2.1.86

Blackbird
Song Thrush
Mistle Thrush
Blue Tit
Great Tit
Greenfinch
Bullfinch
Wren
Robin
House Sparrow
Dunnock
Starling
Pied Wagtail
Black Headed gull.

6th January 1986

For my first visit to the countryside in 1986 I went to the meadow alongside the Warren in Hutton Village, where I was able to make some sketches of the horses. It was overcast and very cold, only 5°c and so I had to work quickly.

There were ten horses in the field, all but two heavy shires with varying colours of Black, Brown and White. One of the largest, a rather untidy but very lovable black shire was especially friendly, nosing into my material bag and then onto my sketch paper while I worked. He left a dirty mark alongside my drawing but it mattered little as I was going to do the sketches again anyway, in my much warmer room at home.

For the hour that I stayed in the meadow the same 'scruffy' shire was never far from me, spending much of the time just looking at me. His placid stance hiding the immense power harnessed in his limbs. I had nothing to give him but the next day I returned to feed them all some apples.

Piebald Pony

J Marriott
8.1.86

98

Horses in a meadow
at
Hutton Village

Grazing

Looking at me

This brown and
white shire was
rather timid,
but was the first
to eat my apples.

J. Merriott.
7.1.86.

Long Tail Tits.

J Merriott
11-1-86

6th January 1986

It is very often the case when persuing a particular feature of the countryside that something extra is seen. So it was with the long tail tits that I saw in the same field as where I was sketching the horses. I counted eight very high up in the tall bare trees, flicking from twig to twig, sometimes hanging topsy turvey in their search for food.

11th January 1986

Collared Dove

The constant attention paid to the bird table by the smaller birds attracted collared Doves into the garden today. There were four, one landing in the christmas tree, others on the lawn and on the roof of the bird table. They were however too nervous to go where the food was, put off by the presence of the roof over the feeding area.

J Merriott
21.1.86

Thorndon Country Park

J. Merriott
18·1·86

Gateway to Thorndon — 18th January 1986

    On the day that I saw the fox at Thorndon Park over the christmas holiday, I made up my mind to return as quickly as possible to sketch this lovely arrangement of the stile alongside the gate and the nameboard, as my introduction to the park. It was an inspiring afternoon and although only 3-o-clock when I started, within the hour the night had began to move in, highlighted by the red in the sky.

Thoughts of Thorndon.

Although it is no more than five years since I first came to Thorndon Park, it is as if I have been coming here all my life. The landscape being typical of all that is best of the English countryside.

If people find an attraction to it's landscape then wildlife finds an attraction in it's environment. A variety of habitat ranging from woodland grassland and marshland, with the addition of two lakes reserved for nature, is connected by pathways and bridleways and is home for a vast variety of fauna and flora.

There are no cultivated flower beds here, just a saturation of country park flowers and grasses fringing the walkways, and in springtime carpeting a woodland of oak and hornbeam.

Birds are abundant with summer visitors congregating to what appears to be proportions of over popularity. The more common of the wild animals are an every day encounter and a fair range of reptiles includes snakes and lizards. One thing however above all else brings me back on at least two dozen occasions every year – the Butterflies. Conducting a habitat survey since 1983 has resulted in recordings of 26 species including the rare White letter hairstreak and the migrant clouded yellow. It is the butterflies that keep me hanging on when I should have been on my homeward journey hours before.

God willing I shall always return to this glorious place which I have the good fortune to live so close to

19-1-86

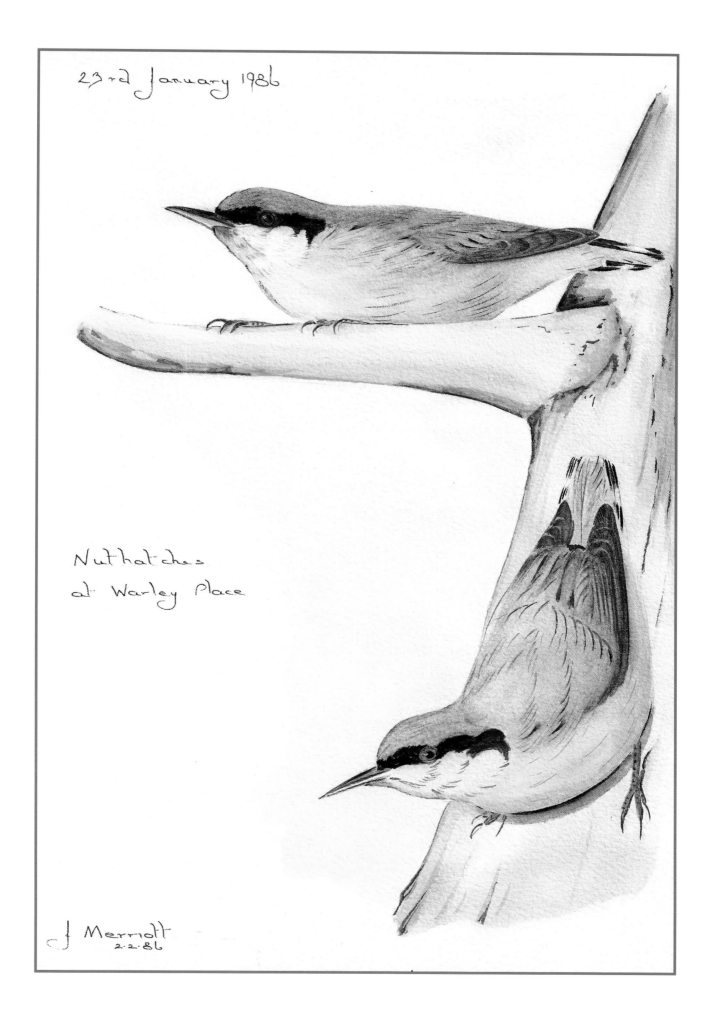

23rd January 1986

Nuthatches
at Warley Place

J Merriott
2.2.86

Rabbit

Warley Place 23rd January 1986

The very beautiful nature reserve known as Warley Place in Brentwood is most impressive for it's wild flowers. No flowers to be seen in mid winter however, but this time of the year the impact is created by the trees, particularly the enormous beach trees. It was in the beach trees that Julie and I saw the Nuthatches. There were four in all, that we were able to watch for some time when we visited during the afternoon. In addition to the birds we also saw squirrels and watched rabbits from the hide by the pond.

Grey Squirrel

J. Merriott
1.2.86.

105

24th January 1986.

On Sunday last Greensted Church was featured in a documentary television programme, "You can't see the wood for the Trees", with David Bellamy. The oldest wooden church in the world, St Andrews - Greensted has in the past, featured in other T.V. programmes, it has been disguised as a 'mastermind' question and has been the subject of a postage stamp. Yet in almost twenty years of living in Brentwood I had never been to see it, even though it is no more than a twenty minute drive from where I live.

Today I made time, and during some lovely afternoon winter sunshine I made my first visit to this historic place. I never lost sight of the fact that here was a place of worship but never-the-less allowed myself the pleasure of becoming overjoyed with it's complete charm.

I sat in the churchyard and started a line and wash drawing but after half an hour was to cold to continue and so completed it at home. My daughter said she liked the church drawn in ink before I washed in the colour, and so I did another.

'St Andrews' church — Greensted Ongar Essex.   JM 28:86

18th February 1986
Black headed Gulls

J Merriott
25·2·86

Apparently unaffected by the intense February cold. By mid-month, many Blackheaded Gulls, seen around my garden, were in breeding plumage.

The sufferings of wildlife during what has turned out to be the prolonged 'arctic' February, is to some extent compensated in that the wild creatures become so close. Today I ventured out for the first time this month, going for a local drive with brief stops at Hutton Village, Childerditch Common and Thorndon Park.

21st February 1986
Moorhen

J. Merriott
26.2.86

Before I left home I counted 7 Bullfinches in a nearby front garden and as I drove through the village, a Moorhen, so often so quick to recede to cover on better days, stood motionless by the roadside, moving only when a fast car passed. Later, a vixen fox sighted on Childerditch Common was also quite unconcerned by my close attentions and went quietly along her way.

When I returned home the chestnut tree on the opposite side of the road was being occupied by half dozen or more long tail tits, behaving as though the sub zero temperatures did not exist.

15th March 1986

A cold foggy week followed the improvement in the weather that occurred last weekend, but changed back again today into what proved a magnificent spring weekend.

Garden wildlife was in its spring mood. The resident female blackbird has removed all last years plant 'debris' from the pond, nest material of course. Frog made an appearance from within the lush pond vegitation with only his head above water. Much bathing occurred with blackbird, blue tit and Robin taking turns. Visitors included dunnock on the lawn, male chaffinch on the garage roof, wren on the covered perching area and the most exciting visitor, a goldcrest spending much time hunting insects in the Ivy over the rustic fence.

The heather was at last at it's best and a sprinkling of yellow crocus were in full bloom. Snowdrops were first seen at Abbess Roding last weekend, but today were a spectacular sight seen in the half light in many local gardens as I cycled to work in the beautiful early evening of this premature spring day.

Spring in Brentwood

Snowdrops.

J. Merriott
16.3.86

109

15th March 1986
Garden - Byron Road.

Frog
Sitting in the goldfish pond.

Female Blackbird
collecting nest material

Goldcrest.
among Ivy

J. Merriott
22.3.86

Thorndon Park
9th April 1986

Comma

This comma butterfly, which I disturbed from its thorny roost, was the first seen in 1986 and was therefore the first butterfly painted in this book.

Small Tortoiseshells
J. Merriott
12·4·86

Two small Tortoiseshell butterflies were also disturbed, when Julie approached where they were resting amid last years plant debris.

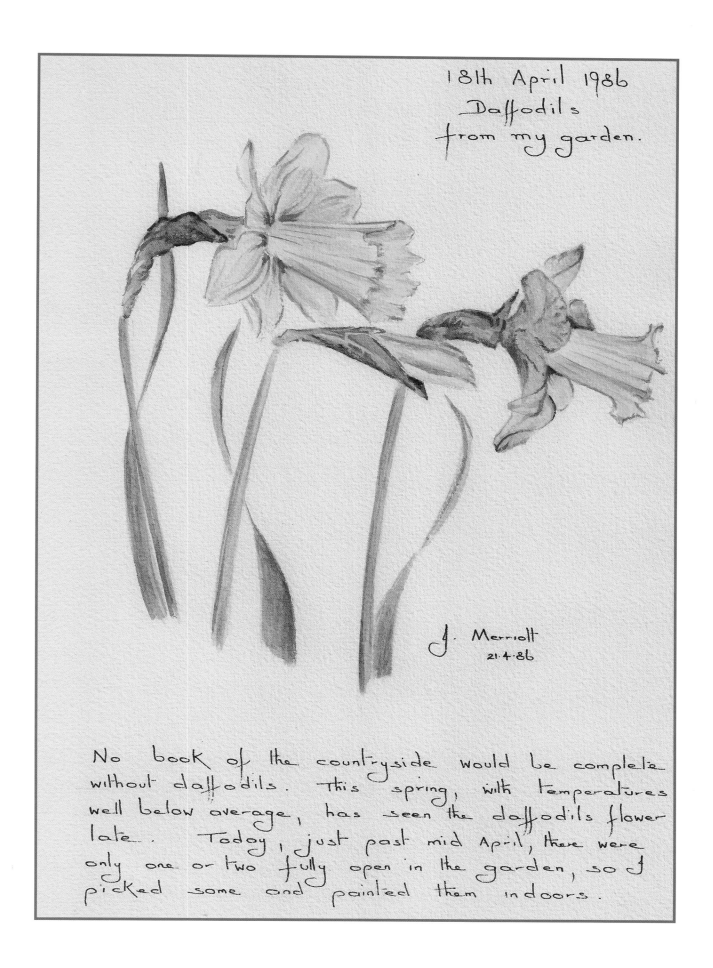

18th April 1986
Daffodils
from my garden.

J. Merriott
21.4.86

No book of the countryside would be complete
without daffodils. This spring, with temperatures
well below average, has seen the daffodils flower
late. Today, just past mid April, there were
only one or two fully open in the garden, so I
picked some and painted them indoors.

Blue Tits in The Garden.

9th April 1986
Pair of Blue Tits
commenced occupation
of the nest box in
the garden

The female
frequently
entered the
box and looked
out through the
entrance hole

The male behaves
very aggressive to
'intruders'. Occasionally
he 'peeks' into box.

10th April 1986
Female
started to
take in nest
material
(bits of
dried grass
collected)

J. Merriott
14.4.86

Hutton Village - 1st May 1986

Following the cold winter and uncertain spring, May arrived in a blaze of sunshine. Over the past few days the temperature has risen daily to reach a splendid 20°c today, the first day of May.

I went for an hour long walk through Hutton Village where spring life was blooming as if there had been no hold up by the cold wet spring.

Sightings included my first Peacock and first Small White Butterflies of the year and the first summer visiting birds of the season. A House Martin was seen in the Warren and in the large old oak which stands on the corner of the village at Hall Green Lane, a Garden Warbler was seen.

Details of some of the sightings is as follows:-
Total Butterflies = 6 Small Tortoise shell. 4 Small White
2 Peacock and 1 Comma (seen in the Warren)

Some of the flowers seen in bloom = Speedwell. Hawkweed, Dandelion, Daisy, Celendine, chickweed, Red-dead nettle, coltsfoot, Greater stitchwort and in my garden - Violet.

J. Merriott
10.5.86

Garden Warbler
Visitor to Hutton from the South!

114

1st May 1986

Small White

The Small White feeding from blossom of Blackthorn was a delightful sight seen in church Lane.

Peacock

Because it was later into the year than usual before my first sighting of this most magnificent butterfly, the thrill was bigger for the wait.

Violets growing wild in my garden.

J. Merriott
11.5.86.

J Merriott
13·5·86

House Martin.

Although they arrive from the south a
little later than the swallows, when I
saw my first House Martin of the season
flying above Hutton Warren on the first
day of May, I had yet to see a swallow

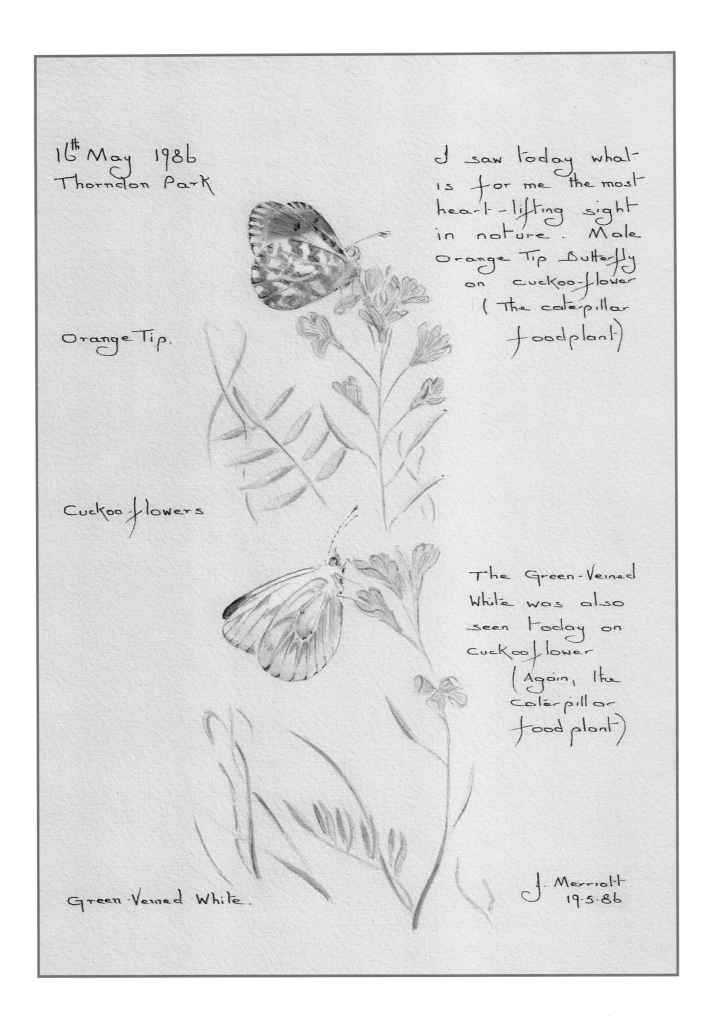

16th May 1986
Thorndon Park

I saw today what
is for me the most
heart-lifting sight
in nature. Male
Orange Tip Butterfly
on cuckoo-flower
(The caterpillar
foodplant)

Orange Tip.

Cuckoo-flowers

The Green-Veined
White was also
seen today on
Cuckoo flower
(Again, the
Caterpillar
food plant)

Green-Veined White.

J. Merriott
19·5·86

The male Brimstone
and the female
Large White
flew past me and
then away.
I did not
see either
land.

Brimstone.

Large White.

Eight species
of Butterflies
were seen at
Thorndon Park
today 16.5.86

1/ Orange Tip
2/ Brimstone
3/ Large White
4/ Small White
5/ Green-veined White
6/ Small Tortoiseshell
7/ Peacock
8/ Comma.

J. Merriott
21-5-86

Brentwood
21st May 1986

J. Merriott
25.5.86

The Hutton Heron

Seen on a number
of occasions over the
past couple of years,
the Heron was seen
again over Byron Road today.
Looking very ragged, his tatty
wings were showing gaps between
the primaries as he flew across
the early evening sky. Behind him,
higher up, a swift, many of which
have been seen during the past week.

The
Old Cottage
Sussex

J. Merriott
5.6.86

120

Moths in May

Among the moths seen during the time spent in Sussex were these four, all of which were seen flying during the daytime.

Speckled Yellow Moth.
Normanhurst Court   26th May 1986

Cinnabar Moth
South downs near Lullington   29th May 1986

Brimstone Moth
Beachy Head   30th May 1986

Buff-Tip Moth
Normanhurst court   27th May 1986

J. Merriott
9-6-86

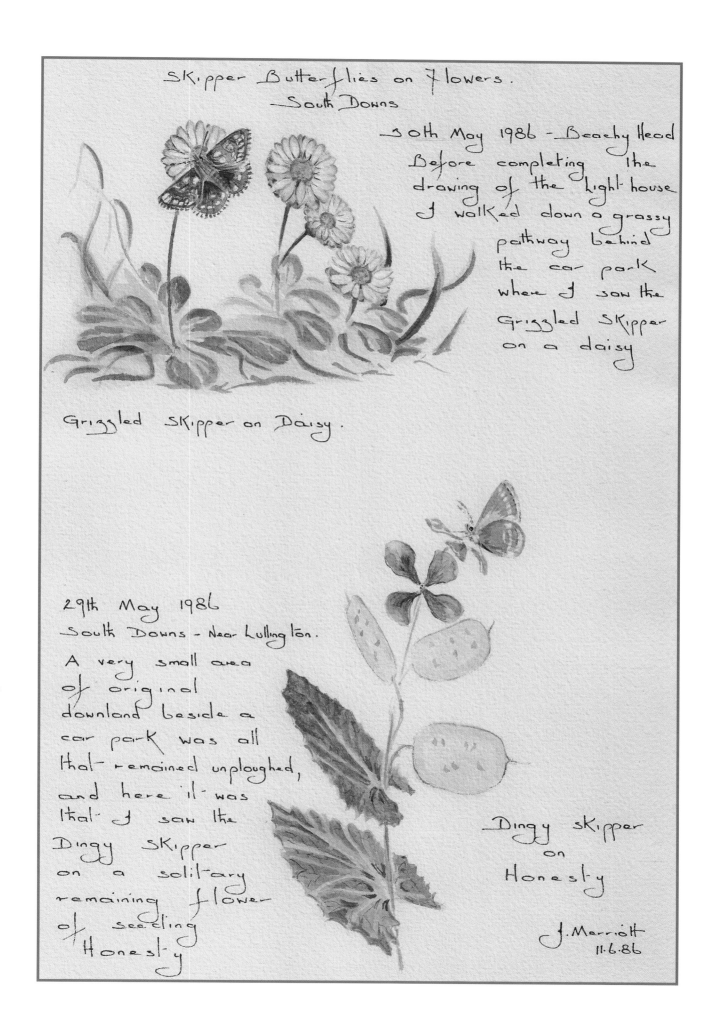

Skipper Butterflies on Flowers.
South Downs

30th May 1986 - Beachy Head
Before completing the
drawing of the light-house
I walked down a grassy
pathway behind
the car park
where I saw the
Griggled Skipper
on a daisy

Griggled Skipper on Daisy.

29th May 1986
South Downs - Near Lullington.

A very small area
of original
downland beside a
car park was all
that remained unploughed,
and here it was
that I saw the
Dingy Skipper
on a solitary
remaining flower
of seedling
Honesty

Dingy skipper
on
Honesty

J. Marriott
11.6.86

More Butterflies in Sussex. 26.5.86 to 31.5.86

(Other sightings during week.)

Large White

Small White

Green Veined White

Orange Tip

Brimstone

Comma.

Speckled Wood.
Seen in the woods
surrounding
Normanhurst Court
27.5.86

Yellow Pimpernel.
Growing just a
short distance from the
caravan, Normanhurst
Court. Found 26.5.86

Holly Blue — Normanhurst
Court   28-5-86

Small Copper.
Beachy Head
30.5.86

Red Admiral.
In flight by the caravan.
Normanhurst Court — 30.5.86

J. Marriott
21.6.86

Brentwood — By the railway embankment.
2 nd June 1986

Slow Worm.

J. Merriott
21.6.86

Returning from work in the evening J came face to face with a slow worm as J cycled along the pathway alongside the Shenfield railway embankment. He was in a very precarious position and being quite unable to move at any pace, he just remained where he was putting himself in my trust. Without touching him, J prompted him to return to the cover of the undergrowth. J was surprised at the difficulty he found in getting moving but he eventually reached safety and J watched him slide away through the lengthy grass. J was impressed with the bright golden colour of his skin.

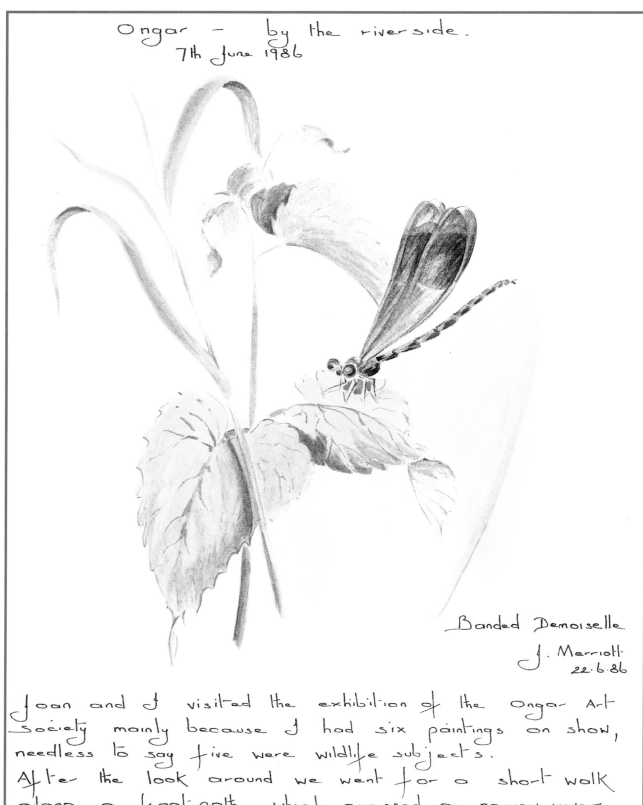

Ongar — by the riverside.
7th June 1986

Banded Demoiselle
J. Merriott
22.6.86

Joan and I visited the exhibition of the Ongar Art
Society mainly because I had six paintings on show,
needless to say five were wildlife subjects.
After the look around we went for a short walk
along a foot-path which crossed a narrow river.
Joan brought my attention to a beautiful Banded
Demoiselle Damselfly which she saw land in a
bed of stinging nettles inter-growing with rich
green grasses.

Meadow in Billericay
14th June 1986
Common Blue
(on
Meadow Buttercup)
and Small Heath.
Butterflies.

J. Merriott
26.6.86

Denbies Hillside
23rd June 1986
Adonis Blue
Butterflies
(Male and Female)
on
Horseshoe Vetch.

J. Merriott
28·6·86

Denbies Hillside
23-rd June 1986.

I saw a thousand or
more fragrant orchids
growing in huge banks
over the hillside but
found only one solitary
Bee orchid.

Also seen today, the
first of the summer
skippers - A Large
skipper.

Bee Orchid

Large Skipper Butterfly

J. Merriott
6.7.86

Thrift Wood - Danbury
27th June 1986

Successful introduction of the
Heath Fritillary Butterfly.

On the same day I saw:-
The rarest
British Butterfly......

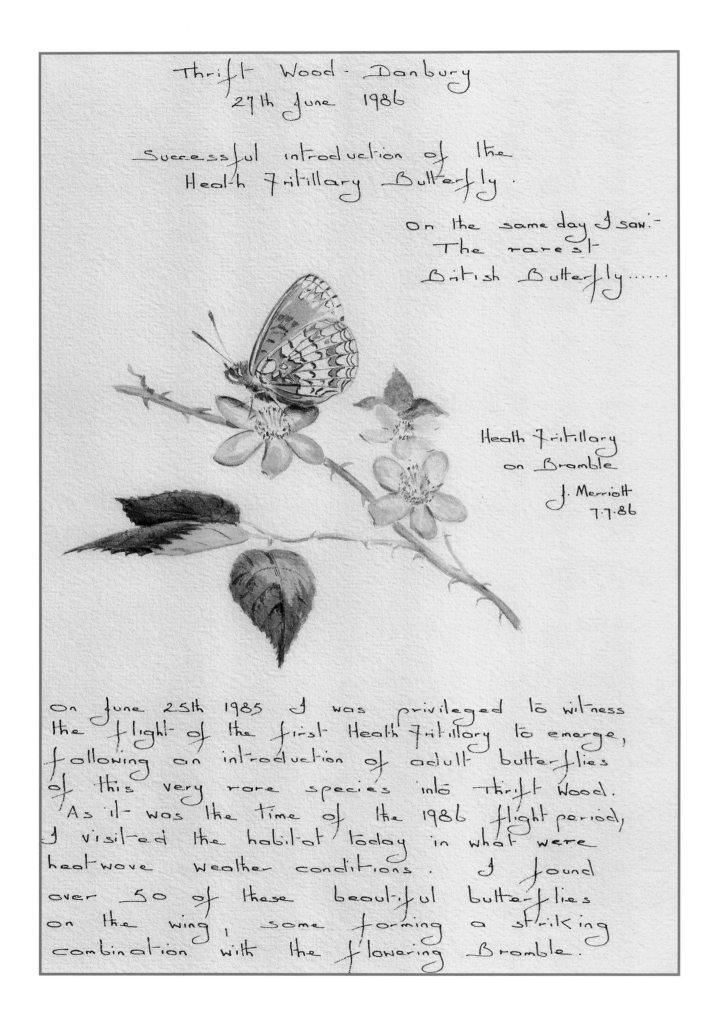

Heath Fritillary
on Bramble
J. Merriott
7.7.86

On June 25th 1985 I was privileged to witness the flight of the first Heath Fritillary to emerge, following an introduction of adult butterflies of this very rare species into Thrift Wood. As it was the time of the 1986 flight period, I visited the habitat today in what were heatwave weather conditions. I found over 50 of these beautiful butterflies on the wing, some forming a striking combination with the flowering Bramble.

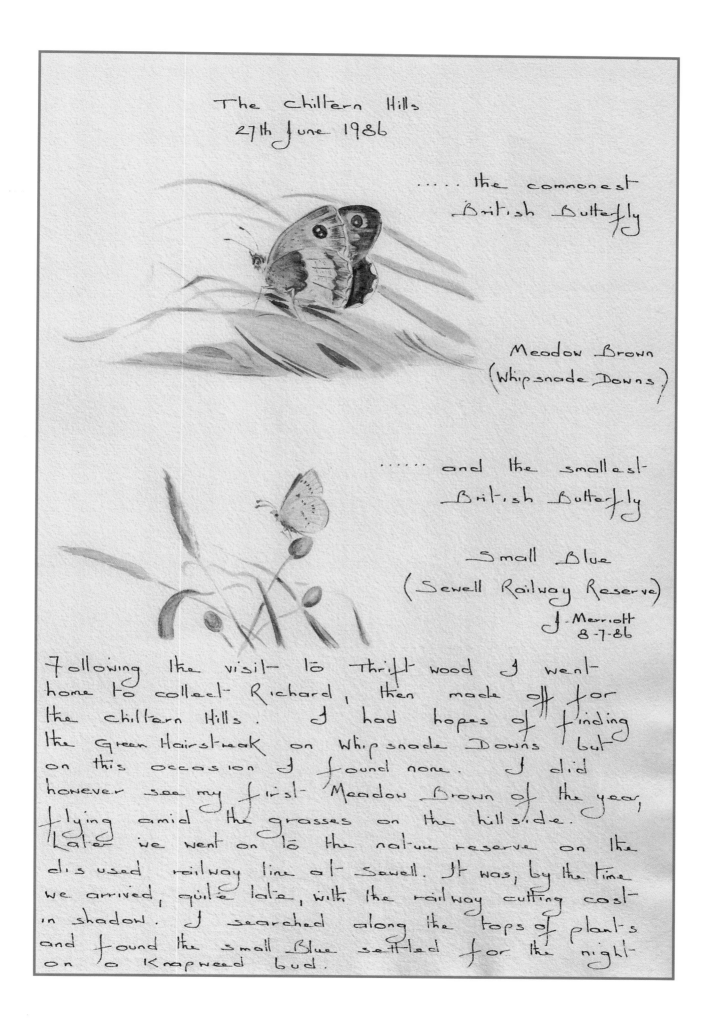

The Chiltern Hills
27th June 1986

..... the commonest
British Butterfly

Meadow Brown
(Whipsnade Downs)

...... and the smallest
British Butterfly

Small Blue
(Sewell Railway Reserve)
J. Merriott
8-7-86

Following the visit to Thrift wood I went
home to collect Richard, then made off for
the Chiltern Hills. I had hopes of finding
the Green Hairstreak on Whipsnade Downs but
on this occasion I found none. I did
however see my first Meadow Brown of the year,
flying amid the grasses on the hillside.
Later we went on to the nature reserve on the
disused railway line at Sewell. It was, by the time
we arrived, quite late, with the railway cutting cast
in shadow. I searched along the tops of plants
and found the Small Blue settled for the night
on a Knapweed bud.

130

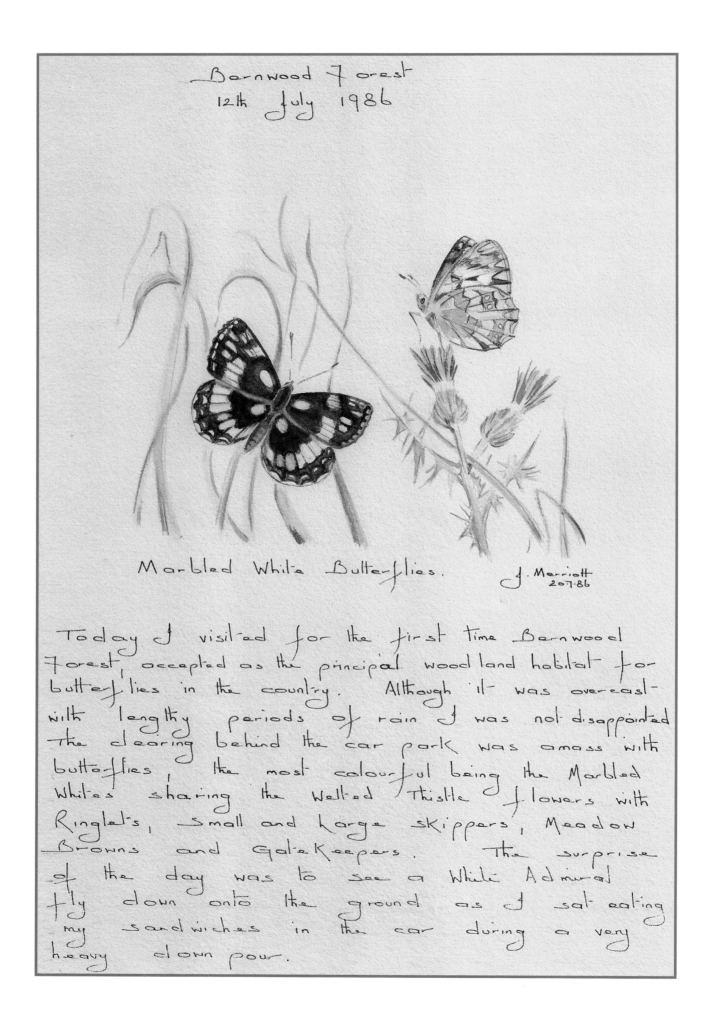

Barnwood Forest
12th July 1986

Marbled White Butterflies.

J. Merriott
20.7.86

Today I visited for the first time Barnwood Forest, accepted as the principal woodland habitat for butterflies in the country. Although it was overcast with lengthy periods of rain I was not disappointed. The clearing behind the car park was amass with butterflies, the most colourful being the Marbled Whites sharing the Welted Thistle flowers with Ringlets, small and large skippers, Meadow Browns and Gatekeepers. The surprise of the day was to see a White Admiral fly down onto the ground as I sat eating my sandwiches in the car during a very heavy downpour.

Bernwood Forest.
12th July 1986
Summer Butterflies.

Small Skipper
on Welted Thistle

Gate Keeper
on Welted Thistle

Ringlet

White Admiral.
Which came down onto
the 'chippings' in the
car park during a
heavy shower

J. Merriott.
16.7.86.

Denbies Hillside
22 nd. July 1986

Silver Washed Fritillary
J. Merriott
2.8.86

Accompanied by Richard I made my second visit of the season to Denbies Hillside. My priority was to see what for me belongs more than anything else upon a chalk down – the Chalkhill Blue Butterfly. Only the males were out and we saw around ten, the dusty pale blue of their wings blending perfectly into their chalky environment. Above where the Chalkhill Blues were flying, a large area of hillside massed with Knapweed was 'saturated' with Marbled Whites and skippers, with more than just a few Dark Green Fritillaries, another butterfly that I had come especially to see. Additionaly there was a surprise, a Silver Washed Fritillary which I did not expect to find enjoyed the bramble blossom at the edge of some trees.

Denbies Hillside
22nd July 1986

Dark Green Fritillary
on Knopweed

Chalkhill Blue
on Marjoram

J. Merriott.
3·8·86

134

J Merriott
14.8.86

Wild Flowers of the Cornish hedgerow.

135

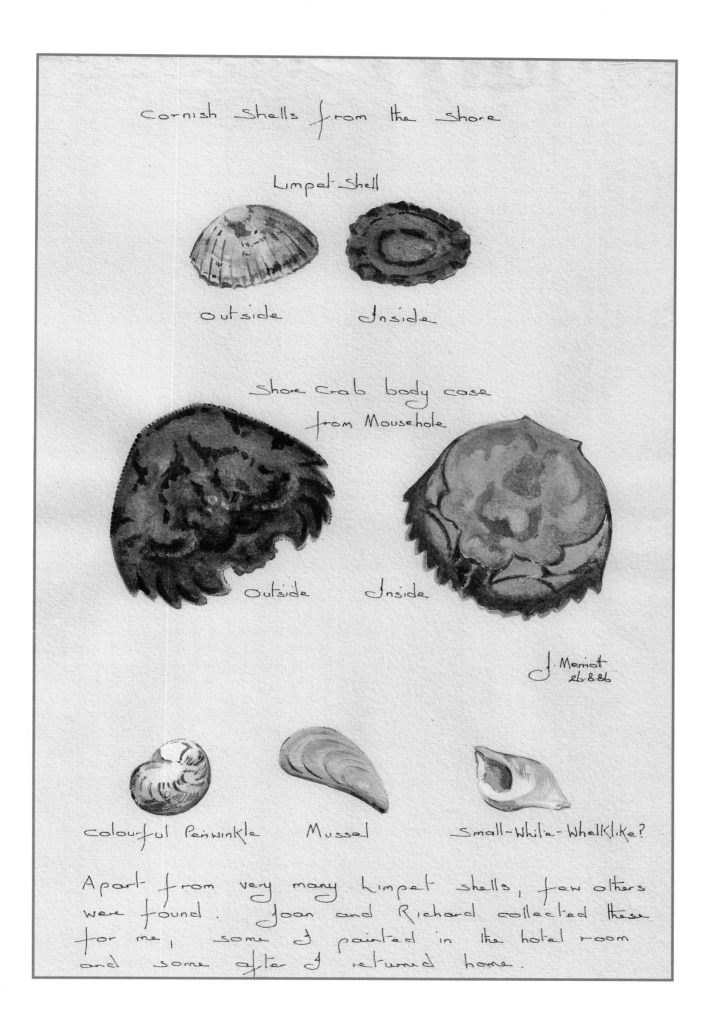

Cornish Shells from the Shore

Limpet Shell

Outside   Inside

Shore Crab body case
from Mousehole

Outside   Inside

J. Merriott
26.8.86

colourful Periwinkle   Mussel   Small-While-Whelk-like?

Apart from very many limpet shells, few others were found. Joan and Richard collected these for me, some I painted in the hotel room and some after I returned home.

CHAPTER 9

FRIENDS AND HEROES

One man's lifetime, is not long enough to amass too many lasting impressions of friends and heroes, which is probably just as well as I do tend 'to go on a bit' at times. So I shall try to be brief and place them in no particular order.

John Valentine Alder 1923 – 1991. Although I never knew it at the time, outside my wife and family, John was the best friend I ever had. We worked together for 8 years at Ford Motor Company's Becket House in Brentwood, Essex.

Our job was to look after the premises and its occupants, but we did have lots of time to relate to each other and I learned so much about a side of life so different from my own.

John joined the Royal Navy in 1939, and throughout the war was active on warships in the North Atlantic and what he lovingly termed as 'down in the Med'. His stories of that time were harrowing, but to John it meant he was at sea.

He continued to travel for most of his life, staying somewhere for a while and then moving on. His travels kept him from settling down until the latter part of his life, but he did marry twice, both times to the same girl, the beautiful Iris, who had been his childhood sweetheart.

Sadly John never wrote a book, but part of his legacy is his wonderful poetry.

THE WANDERER

I've sailed the mighty ocean
Under billowing sail and steam
I've circled the world about nine times
Which to some may seem extreme

I'm a wandering guy, with a roving eye
And a pair of itchy feet
But it's not the place or the distance
It's the wonderful people I meet

There are a few who envy me
And would join me when I go
To far flung corners of the Earth
Where unchartered waters flow

But there is always the solid citizen
Whose life is pretty small
He stays in his own little corner
And rarely moves at all

A waster sir, neer-do-well
He is inclined to sneer
He's positive that my way of life
Is debauchery, Tobacco and Beer

But should we pause and think a while
Go back to the start of time
Because of those men with itchy feet
He has learned of the Gin and Lime

So my friend I say to you
When someday we shall meet
Your comfortable little corner
Was made by our itchy feet.

John Valentine Alder

GLADS COTTAGE – ALDBURY – HERTFORDSHIRE

GEORGE S. TAYLOR

George I have known for only a short time and he has become a close friend for many reasons, but two in particular; the poem 'Jim' that starts this book and his beautiful words at the end. Thanks George for your wonderful contribution.

JIMMY GREAVES

BORN 1940

If I were a football coach, my tactical plan would be, "kick the football into the goal" The professional coaches would argue 'it's not that simple' and of course it isn't, but one man in the history of the game was head and shoulders above everybody else at scoring goals. He did exactly what football is all about; he kicked the ball into the goal.

Jimmy remains, in my opinion the greatest goal scorer the world has ever seen. He 'jinked and jerked' pushed forward, touched and tapped, always or nearly always with the same result, kicking the football into the goal.

The absolute master, the complete artist, he did what is essential to achieve perfection, to do it the simple way, which is always so hard to achieve.

THE BAKERS SHOP – MANNINGTREE – ESSEX

MIKE HAILWOOD

02-04-1940 – 23-03-1981

Revered by fellow competitors past and present as the greatest Motor Cycle Road Racer of all time. 'Mike the bike' was of my time, and I watched his master class on many occasions. He could ride anything, anywhere, and almost always – Win. An ambassador for his sport and his country, I rate him the greatest sportsman of his day.

Not wanting to leave Mike out on his own, I shall add the names of three more men of my time. They performed on a racing motorcycle with breathtaking ability outside the realms of what is humanly possible, they were superhuman. Derek Minter, John Cooper and Phil Read – just three of many.

It was a great privilege not to only watch them, but also exhilarating to be out there racing among them.

BOB DYLAN

BORN 23rd MAY 1941

Poet, painter, storyteller, legend writer, Bob Dylan does all these things, but with magical and extraordinary words.

Amazingly the lyrics written over 50 years ago just went on and on. As Joan Baez put it, 'he just sits at the typewriter and the words pour out like tic-a-tape. What words they are, masterpieces of rhyme, and he's still out there finding more wonderful lyrics. One of his band members summed him up. "God sometimes taps someone on the shoulder and gives them a talent".

HIGH STREET RESTAURANT – BILLERICAY – ESSEX

PIERRE AUGUSTE RENOIR

25-02-1841 – 02-12-1919

So many accolades have been bestowed upon the immortal Renoir, I can only add he is my absolute hero. Although in his early life he experienced poverty and war, his strong belief in the beauty of life saw him through. He would be the one man outside my lifetime that I would loved to have met, not only because of his miraculous paintings, but also because he was such a joyous person. He left the world with his ultimate vision of timeless beauty.

Pierre Auguste Renoir – My greatest hero. Even his name sounds like a beautiful melody.

VIEW FROM THE EIGHTH

I look eastwards to the horizon
At my back is the setting sun
I observe the bustle in the streets below
Of the worker when day is done

I lose myself in the atmosphere
Reminded of the things far away
The fertile plains of India
Or the view from Frisco's bay

I can see the hills where the trees once stood
Casting shade over bubbling streams
And flowers that bloomed on the fertile banks
Where lovers planned their dreams

Alas, this beauty has been removed
The path of progress laid
They have to build so well and grim
For there's money to be made

As I return from my reverie
The scene is cold and stark
No more the trees or humming bees
Not even a little park

Instead there is the big highway
A wound in nature's side
Of flashing lights and ghastly smells
And noise where death does ride

Oh God there must be some place
That progress hasn't struck
Where a man enjoys the natural things
Without freezer, fast car or truck

Perhaps my search is a hopeless cause
But I think that someday soon
I will find a place in natures arms
Just the trees the Sun and Moon.

John Valentine Alder

WIVENHOE BOOKSHOP – WIVENHOE – ESSEX

COTTAGE ON THE CORNER – BARKWAY – HERTFORDSHIRE

143

ALL SAINTS CHURCH – HUTTON

CHAPTER 10

PAINTING TECHNIQUE

So much information is available on watercolour painting technique; there isn't much that I feel is necessary to add. I will however make some suggestions that I hope will help.

Firstly, I am self taught, and found trial and error a great way to learn, because mistakes are not easily forgotten, and lead to positive steps to overcome them.

For each watercolour I carry out three defined procedures:

1 – I draw with a pencil (**2B**) on the watercolour paper as much as is necessary to show me where to put the paint.

2 – I thoroughly wet the surface of the paper, leaving any white areas dry, and then add a wash of colour which finishes the sky and establishes 'undercolour' to the remaining parts.

3 – I then draw the whole thing again, but this time with paint and brush instead of pencil.

The best lesson I believe is to look at the work of a good water-colourist and learn from what you see.

Remember, very few if any water-colourists are ever satisfied with their results, so don't be disappointed, keep going – **success will come**......

HAPPY PAINTING!

RIVER LEA – LEMSFORD – HERTFORDSHIRE

THE OLD FORGE – BARLEY – HERTFORDSHIRE

COTTAGE IN TRING ROAD – WILSTONE – HERTFORDSHIRE

THE INGLENOOK – GT. GADDESDEN – HERTFORDSHIRE

COTTAGE IN STOCKS ROAD – ALDBURY – HERTFORDSHIRE

RIVERSIDE COTTAGE – GT. SAMPFORD – ESSEX

OLD WORLD COTTAGE – PAGLESHAM – ESSEX

FINCHINGFIELD ROAD – GT. SAMPFORD – ESSEX

CHAPTER 11

LIVING WITH JIM

We had only been married 4 years when we were given the news that Jim had Rheumatoid Arthritis, and what a shock it was to us both! Our daughter Julie was 3 years old and had just started playschool. A very bubbly child who thought nothing of getting dad to lift her high up and 'doing tricks' as she called out excitedly, "Olay-like in the circus daddy". Jim was finding it hard even then to live a normal life, but carried on regardless, going to work every day to Shoreditch Fire Station. He loved his job, but knew that one day it would come to an end. He went through the ranks and became a Station Officer towards the end of his career, being transferred to Brigade Headquarters and a desk job until retirement.

POST OFFICE AND VILLAGE STORES – POTTEN END – HERTFORDSHIRE

Life was becoming much harder for him as the disease progressed, so much so, that he was wondering how on earth he was to support his family. Then our second child Richard had been born, who was hyper active, (I knew the day he was conceived just how hyper !!!). We used to say, when Richard finally went to sleep, 'He's charging his batteries ready for tomorrow'. Julie by now was 9 years old, and was a little mum to Richard as much as me. I will always remember, when he would knock into Jim by mistake in his hurry to do whatever he was doing, and Jim would scream with the pain. Richard would say 'sorry dad, sorry dad, does it hurt? It will all be better soon!!!

Jim was beginning to suffer really badly, losing weight, always tired, falling asleep the minute he sat down and not really enjoying his food. His Rheumatologist, Dr. Clarke, was adamant that there was something more causing him to be in this condition. He decided to start tests to try and find out what was wrong. After several years of tests, a diagnosis was still to be found. Jim got to a point that he just wanted to be left alone, until one day a diagnosis was found, Jim was Coeliac. All it took was a biopsy.

FIVE CORNERS COTTAGE – FELSTED – ESSEX

From that day on, things began to change; we were put in touch with a nutritionist who gave us lots of information on The Coeliac Society, and how to cope with the disease. Basically, it means a Wheat Free and Gluten Free Diet. From that day on his life changed for the better, and within weeks he regained quite a lot of weight, wasn't tired all the time and had energy again. The now Coelic UK inundated us with many different products, and a book called 'The Food and Drink Directory' that is filled with information from the various supermarket chains and more. The book has made shopping so much easier for me.

Culinary skills had to be changed too, but I must admit it is not the problem I thought it would be. I make his bread in the bread maker, and search out all the ingredients, reading the packets and jars to make sure there is no gluten contained in there.

WELL GREEN – BRAMFIELD – HERTFORDSHIRE

Life has become easier for us, Jim was raring to go. His new love of wild flower meadows had us traipsing all over the southern counties of England searching and photographing them. That wasn't enough for Jim, and he decided to have a go at painting them. His first attempts were very amateurish, but being stubborn he persevered until he got it right; so began his love of painting.

Over the past few years we have had a wonderful time painting together. I'm most certainly never going to get to Jim's standard, but I enjoy it all the same. Life without art, in all forms, would become very boring for us now. To friends I say, *"Life is too short"*, be positive, become a doer.

Joan Merriott

PAPER MILL LOCK – ESSEX

CHAPTER 12

CONCLUSION

From the south facing window of my room, I am greeted each morning with the miracle of light to begin a new day. A new dawn is always the best part of my day, when my mind is filled with optimism of good things to come, anticipating once again the beauty not just today but tomorrow. I do then tend always to look forward and not back. The completing of this book however, has been not just a look back, but a journey back into the past where I have relived in detail so much that has been my life.

One thing above all else has come across to me as the real thrill of my lifetime, People!! My many friends seem to have amassed to cheer me on in my efforts to complete this book. Encouraged me in a way that has left me flabbergasted.

This, then, as I said in the beginning is for you, to share with you, painting companions, art lovers and people;

My Friends
My Dear, Dear Friends

VIEW ACROSS THE MIMRAM VALLEY – BRAMFIELD – HERTFORDSHIRE

I conclude with a poem by John Valentine Alder which he wrote for his wife Iris his childhood sweetheart, the girl he married twice.

MY GIRL, MY WIFE

Her daily chores are never to be envied
She doesn't work from nine to half past three
Her day begins at seven ends around about eleven
That's sixteen hours too much you will agree

Sometimes I stop her in her tracks
Please sit down love and relax
She smiles and says, ok but never does
She just has to be the best that ever was

She makes me coffee makes me tea
Does all the dirty laundry
Finds the time to give us all a little pleasure
Washing nappies, clearing toys, not everyone enjoys
I'm telling you I'm married to a treasure

Some days I'm irritated and everything seems wrong
Then I hear her in the house somewhere
Breaking into song
It makes me feel ashamed that I'm really not that
Strong

She cooks and bakes and scrubs and cleans
Day after day endless it seems
But timelessly she works away
Eye on the kiddies at their play

At last she sits down for a rest
This is time that I like best
Feet on stool in armchair deep
Sometimes she has a little sleep

I wait on her then for a change
A coffee and a snack
We talk about the days that's gone
That will never come back

But there's another day tomorrow
Of it's time we must not borrow
So off to bed my sleepy head
To snuggle close is bliss
It's goodnight love, God bless you dear
Sealed with a loving kiss.

I relate John's words to my wife Joan. Without her I would have achieved nothing.

THE MIDDAY RIDE – DATCHWORTH – HERTFORDSHIRE

ST MARY THE VIRGIN - WALKERN - HERTFORDSHIRE

OLD COTTAGES – CHURCH LANE – GT. MISSENDEN – BUCKINGHAMSHIRE

WHYTE CROFT COTTAGE – HIGH WYCH – HERTFORDSHIRE

One whole lifetime is not long enough to capture a single moment
Claude Oscar Monet
1840-1926

Pleasure and Pain

There are many ways we see and experience life and everyone has their own way of looking at it. Most things are made more enjoyable by their direct opposite, we would not enjoy the sun as much if it was not for rain and we could not have pleasure without pain.

There are of course always exceptions to this rule and one of those is my friend James Merriott. He, like us all, has had many great experiences like racing motorbikes, with the pleasure of speed and competing balanced by the pain of falling off.

Jim however is one of those rare people who have found and given so much pleasure from his pain. The pain of life threatening illness he sees as a positive thing, rather than sitting moaning about it, he feels he is fortunate and indeed lucky to have been given this chance in his life.

Jim paints the most wonderful watercolours and not just by sitting in his studio, he travels far and wide, to paint, teach, give demonstrations and exhibitions, finding great energy and enthusiasm with health limitations that would keep most of us in bed.

I would like to thank Jim sincerely for his help, inspiration and sheer enthusiasm, that has shown me I can do something that, I not only thought I never could, but also for making me want to try.

'I may not have gone where I wanted to go, but I have ended up where I need to be'

G.S.T. November 2010